# KEYS FOR THE KINGDOM™
## Level A

JOSEPH
MARTIN

DAVID
ANGERMAN

MARK
HAYES

Copyright © 1995, GlorySound and Malcolm Music
Divisions of Shawnee Press
International Copyright Secured   All Rights Reserved
Sole Selling Agent: Shawnee Press, Inc.
Delaware Water Gap, PA 18327

H-5001

## Joseph M. Martin

Mr. Martin received his Bachelor of Music in Piano Performance from Furman University, Greenville, South Carolina, and his Master of Music in Piano Performance from the University of Texas, Austin. As a winner of the Nina Plant Wideman Competition, he has performed with symphony orchestras in the United States and Mexico. His solo recital in Ex-convento del Carman, in Guadalajara, Mexico was broadcast nationally throughout that country. As a composer of Christian choral music, Mr. Martin has over 300 compositions published by Shawnee Press and other publishers. He has just completed the recording of his second solo piano album for GlorySound.

Mr. Martin is Director of Church Music Marketing Development at Shawnee Press, and owner of MusiKids, a unique preschool music education program operating in day care centers in several major American cities.

## David Angerman

Mr. Angerman received his Bachelor of Music Education and Master of Music (Church Music) from Baylor University. He also earned a Master of Music in Organ Performance from the University of Texas, Austin. Mr. Angerman's choral and handbell compositions have been published by Shawnee Press and other major publishers, as well as many graded piano solos for the American College of Musicians. He has been teaching piano and organ privately since 1976. Mr. Angerman is a respected adjudicator at choral, handbell, and piano competitions and widely sought after as a workshop clinician and director. He is the Minister of Music at Bethany Lutheran Church in Austin, Texas.

## Mark Hayes

Mr. Hayes earned a Bachelor of Music degree in Piano Performance, *magna cum laude*, from Baylor University. He is well-known for his unique choral settings which reflect his fascination with gospel, jazz, rock, and classical musical styles. His personal catalog includes over 400 published original compositions and arrangements. Mr. Hayes has seven solo piano albums to his credit and is completing his 14th piano book this year.

He has served as an adjunct professor of composition at Midwestern Baptist Theological Seminary in Kansas City, Missouri, and in addition to his involvement in the sacred and secular choral music fields, he is becoming increasingly sought after as an arranger, producer, and solo artist on the contemporary Christian music scene.

## Acknowledgments

The authors gratefully acknowledge the following for their support and special contributions to this project:

**Pamela Martin**, for the special touch you have with words, for capturing a childlike quality in your lyrics, and for the hours you spent in the scriptures finding thoughts that would encourage young lives. Thank you, also, for the hours spent editing and proof-reading, and the way you have given so unselfishly to these efforts and this project.

**Marianne Miller, Illustrator.** Your incredible art brought all of our imaginations to life. Thank you for the gentle beauty you have brought to these books and the sensitivity which so obviously issues from your own faith.

**Cathy Ciccarelli, Shawnee Press Art Director.** Thank you for your eyes and heart for this project. Your patience with us was neverending as we asked all those questions!

**Lew Kirby, Shawnee Press Director of Church Music Publications.** Without your belief in what this series could mean and your tireless efforts on our behalf, *Keys for the Kingdom*™ would not exist.

**Mark Williams**, for your friendship and your special understanding of what music education should and can be. *Viva Musica!*

**The many teachers** all over the country who test-taught *Keys for the Kingdom*™ and gave us invaluable feedback. We are indebted particularly to **Jane Wise** and **Kathy Schmidt** for coordinating these efforts.

**Our fellow church musicians**, many of whom have prayed for us and encouraged us over the years. You are the people who changed our lives by your song. Thank you for allowing us now to sing back to you.

# Contents

# Introduction

Keys for the Kingdom™ is a fully-graded piano series designed especially with the Christian student in mind. Each lesson is carefully written to provide gradual progress. The illustrations are designed to be fun and inspiring, as well as to reinforce the lesson. This graded, multikey, stylistically diverse series of books introduces basic music concepts of rhythm, intervals, scales, chords, music theory, artistry, and improvisation. Companion products include: hymnbooks, contemporary Christian songbooks, theory/technique/improvisation books, performance books, seasonal books, and duet books. These, along with planned future companion materials, will help support the student in his or her learning quest.

The great composer J. S. Bach wrote at the top of many of his compositions In Soli Deo Gloria (to God alone be the glory). It is in that same spirit Keys for the Kingdom™ is written and dedicated. We desire to help inspire the student to achieve his or her personal best in music for the purpose of glorifying God the Creator.

We believe that Keys for the Kingdom™ can be a useful tool for the Christian teacher in a time when motivating a student toward excellence proves to be an increasing challenge. We also hope to encourage the next generation of church musicians and to help the young student discover the joy of serving and praising God through the gift of music.

**Excellence in all things and all things for the glory of God.**

# From Joseph Martin...

The idea for Keys for the Kingdom™ has been a dream of mine for many years. The concept of giving students spiritual support as they develop their skills and understanding of music was something that was an important part of my early life, so I have always wanted to encourage churches and Christian teachers to be involved with music education as part of their outreach and ministry.

When I shared my ideas with Mark Hayes and David Angerman, they joined me in my enthusiasm about such a project as Keys for the Kingdom™ and its potential effectiveness. I have such respect for these men and the work they are doing in sacred and educational music. It has been my privilege to work with these highly creative and deeply-committed Christian musicians.

*Joseph W. Martin*

*P*et the music begin!
Let it sound for God.
Praise Him with your voice.
Praise Him with instruments.
Praise Him with your whole life.
Give your best for His glory!

Based on the Psalms

# Great Beginnings

## Posture at the Keyboard

## Hands on the Keys

# Our Fingers Are Numbered

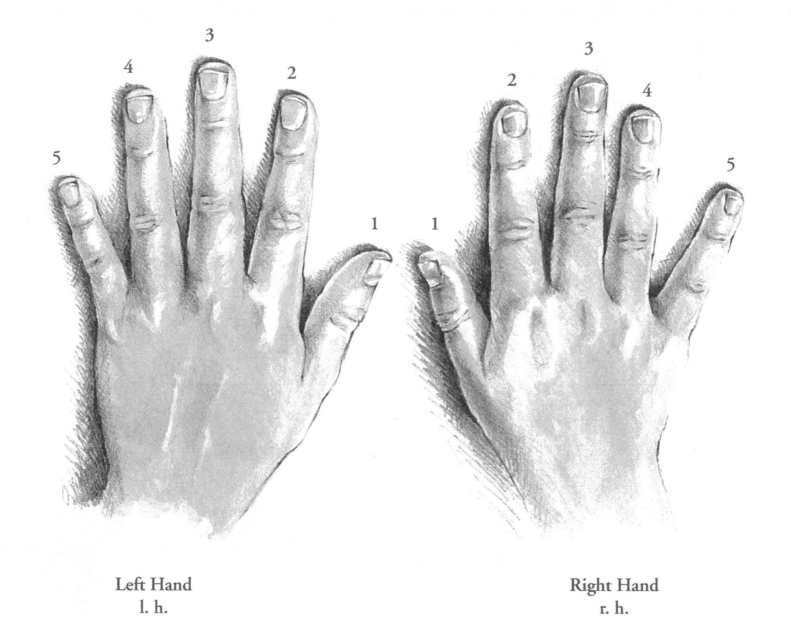

Left Hand
l. h.

Right Hand
r. h.

Trace your own hands on the inside front cover of this book. Label them right and left; then number each finger as shown above.

## Practice Directions

1. Put your hands together like "praying hands." Now tap your "ones" together; tap your "twos" together…and so on.
2. Next, puff out your hands, still keeping your finger tips together as if holding an ostrich egg. Be sure to keep your wrists close together. Now tap your finger tips together as your teacher calls out each finger's number.
3. Place your curved fingers on a table top or the closed lid of the piano and tap the correct fingers as your teacher calls them out.

# Introducing the Black Keys

Notice that all the white keys on the keyboard are side by side, while the black keys are grouped in twos and threes.

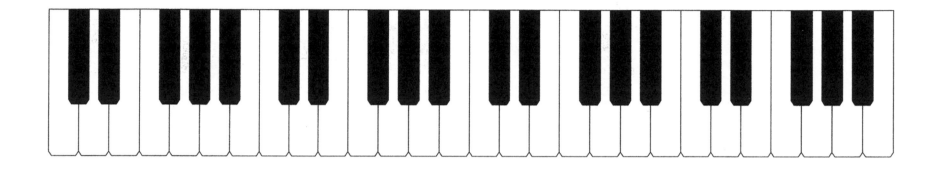

• Find a set of two black keys on your keyboard and play them. Find other two-black-key sets and play them.

• Find a set of three black keys on your keyboard and play them. Find other three-black-key sets and play them.

## Practice Directions

1. Using your right hand, play each two-black-key set going up the keyboard from the cat (middle) to the bird (high).
2. Using your left hand, play each two-black-key set starting with the dog (low) and going up the keyboard to the cat (middle).
3. Using your right hand, play each three-black-key set going down the keyboard from the bird (high) to the cat (middle).
4. Using your left hand, play each three-black-key set going down the keyboard from the cat (middle) to the dog (low).
5. Have your teacher or someone at home call out different groups of black keys for you to play. Examples: "low set of twos" or "middle set of threes" and so on.

# Rhythm in Music
## *Note Values—Quarter Notes and Half Notes*

Rhythm is the combination of long and short tones in music. We show the length of tones in music with different kinds of notes. This is called rhythm.

Quarter note

gets one beat

say:   "one"
or   "quarter"

Half note

gets two beats

say: "one-two"
or "half-note"

Using a set of two black keys, play the rhythm below. Play with each hand separately. Count out loud as you play.

1.

2.

3.

# Bar Lines and Measures

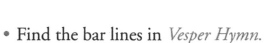 Bar lines divide notes into measures.
A double bar line is used at the end of a song.

bar line        bar line        double bar line

- Find the bar lines in *Vesper Hymn.*
- Trace each bar line with your pencil.
- Draw heart "beats" for every measure.

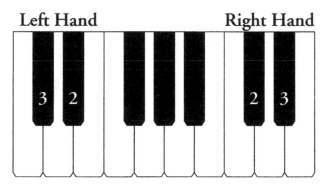

**Left Hand**      **Right Hand**

3 2      2 3

## Practice Directions

1. Play *Vesper Hymn.* Count as you play. Use finger numbers given.
2. Play again and say "right" or "left."

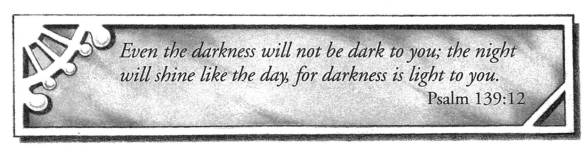

*Even the darkness will not be dark to you; the night will shine like the day, for darkness is light to you.*

Psalm 139:12

14

# VESPER HYMN*

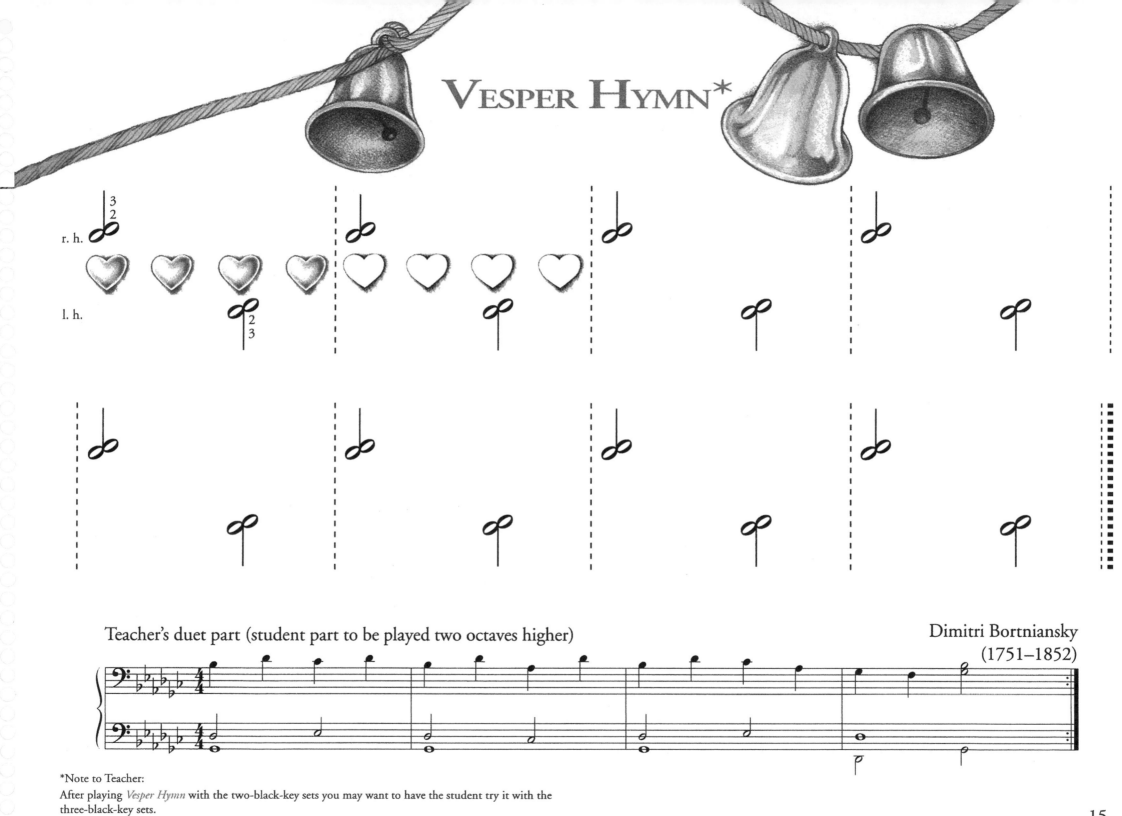

Teacher's duet part (student part to be played two octaves higher)

Dimitri Bortniansky
(1751–1852)

*Note to Teacher:

After playing *Vesper Hymn* with the two-black-key sets you may want to have the student try it with the three-black-key sets.

# Two-Black-Key Set

**Right-Hand Position**

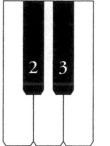

## Practice Directions

1. Sing finger numbers as you play.
2. Count the rhythm as you play.
3. Sing the words as you play.

# AS THE SPARROW

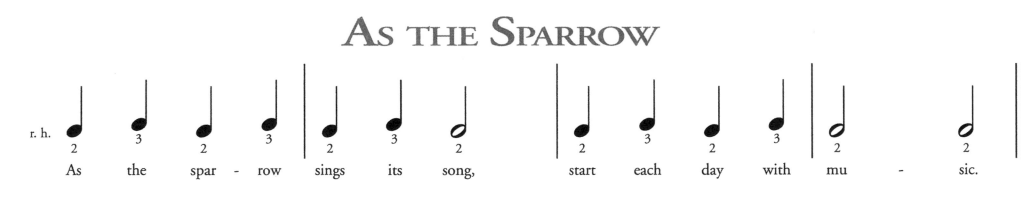

r. h.

| 2 | 3 | 2 | 3 | 2 | 3 | 2 | | 2 | 3 | 2 | 3 | 2 | | 2 |
| As | the | spar | row | sings | its | song, | | start | each | day | with | mu | - | sic. |

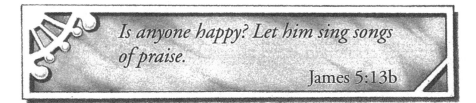

*Is anyone happy? Let him sing songs of praise.*

James 5:13b

# Two-Black-Key Set

## Left-Hand Position

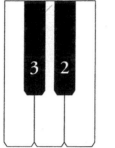

## Practice Directions

1. Sing finger numbers as you play.
2. Count the rhythm as you play.
3. Sing the words as you play.

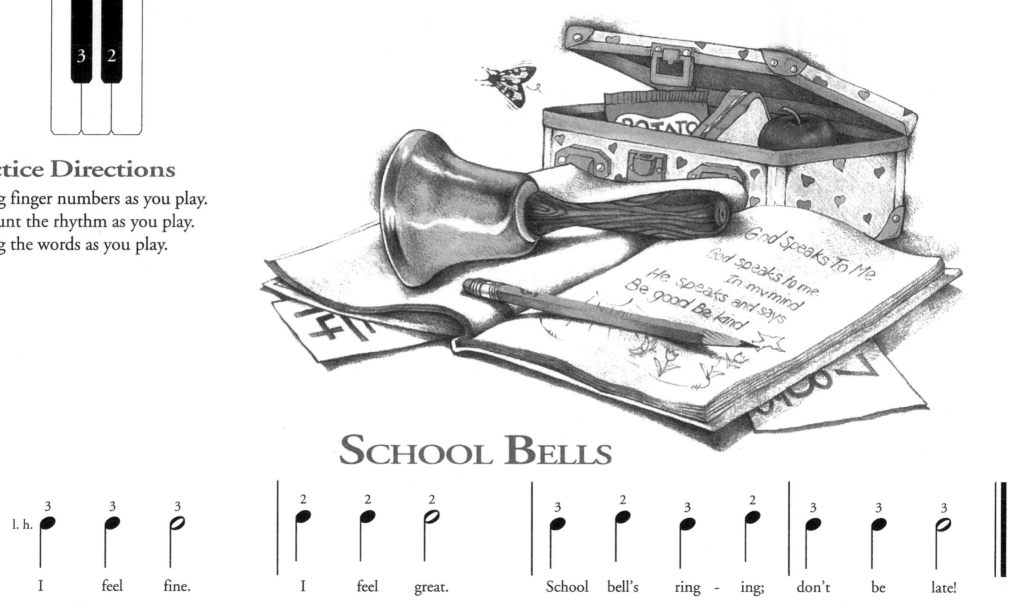

## SCHOOL BELLS

l. h.

| 3 | 3 | 3 | 2 | 2 | 2 | 3 | 2 | 3 | 2 | 3 | 3 | 3 |
|---|---|---|---|---|---|---|---|---|---|---|---|---|
| I | feel | fine. | I | feel | great. | School | bell's | ring- | ing; | don't | be | late! |

# Three-Black-Key Set

## Right-Hand Position

2 3 4

## Practice Directions

1. Sing finger numbers as you play.
2. Count the rhythm as you play.
3. Sing the words as you play.

# OLD MAN NOAH

r. h.

2 3 4 3 2 3 4
Old man No - ah built an ark,

4
3
2
(built an ark, built an ark!)

2 3 4 3 2 3 2
Built it out of go - pher bark,

4
3
2
(go - pher bark, go - pher bark.)

> *By faith, Noah…built an ark to save his family.*
>
> Hebrews 11:7

## Practice Directions*
1. Sing finger numbers as you play.
2. Count the rhythm as you play.
3. Sing the words as you play.

## OLD MAN NOAH

l. h. As the storms raged up a - bove, (up a - bove, up a - bove)

they were safe with - in His love. ('in His love, 'in His love.)

*Note to Teacher:
Beginning with the next song, practice directions will no longer be given unless they differ substantially from the above.

19

# Note Values—Dotted Half Notes

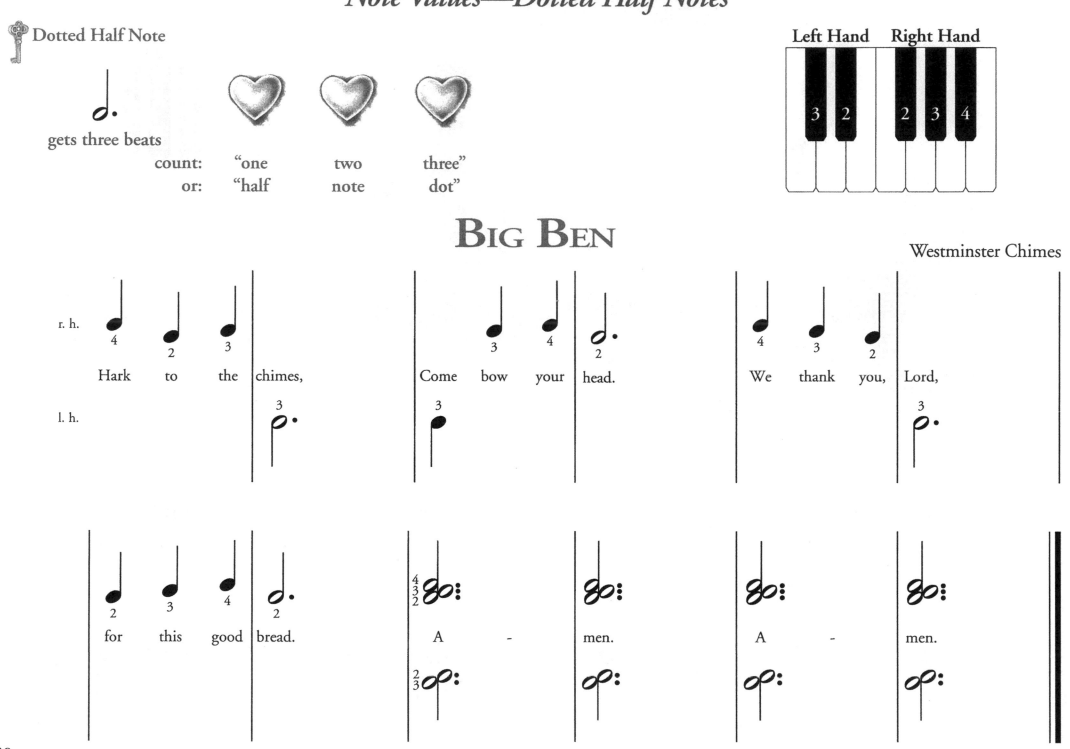

Dotted Half Note

gets three beats

| count: | "one | two | three" |
| or: | "half | note | dot" |

**Left Hand** **Right Hand**

# BIG BEN

Westminster Chimes

r. h.

Hark   to   the   chimes,   Come   bow   your   head.   We   thank   you,   Lord,

l. h.

for   this   good   bread.   A - men.   A - men.

20

## Note Values—Whole Notes

**Whole Note** o gets four beats.

**Repeat Sign** — Play again from the beginning.

Left Hand   Right Hand

# HOLY MANNA*

William Moore (1825)

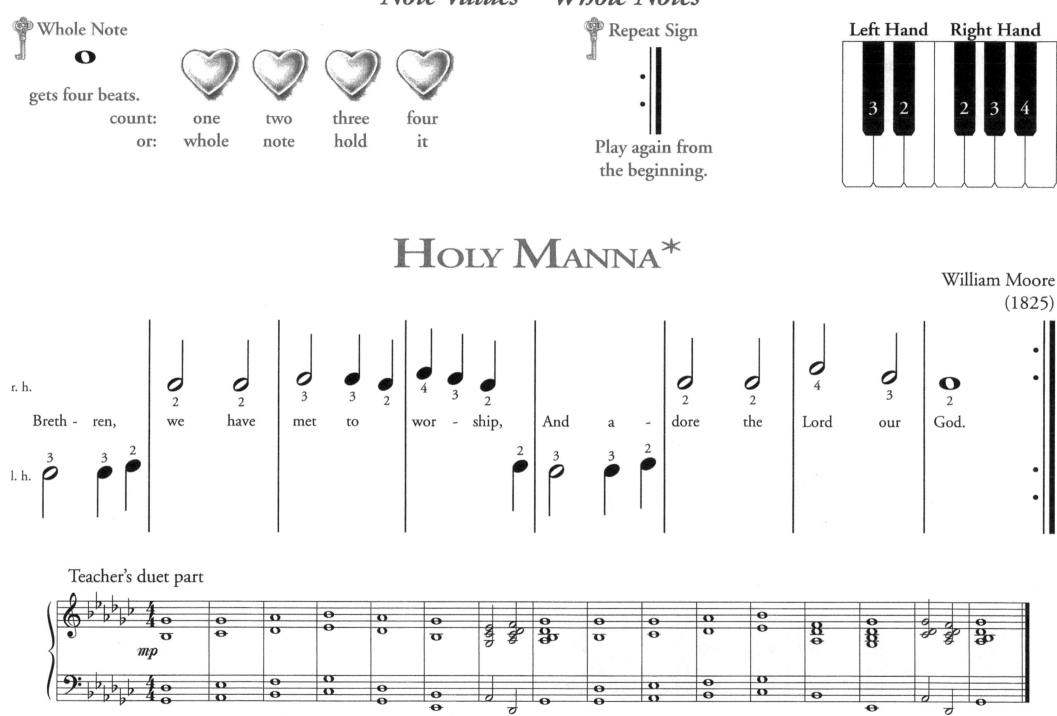

*Manna was the name of the food God gave to the Israelites while they spent forty years wandering in the desert.

# Review No. 1

1. Label each hand with "left hand" and "right hand."
2. Number each finger.

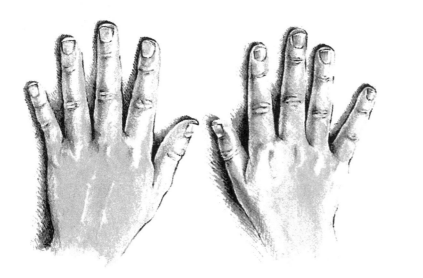

3. Circle all of the two-black-key sets.

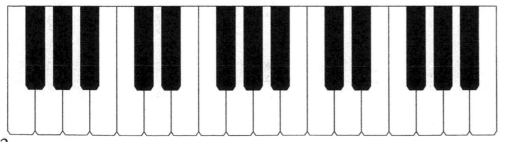

4. Circle all of the three-black-key sets.

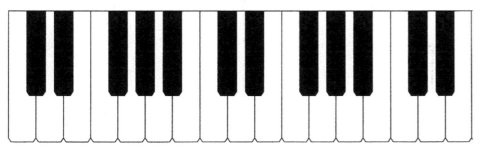

5. Draw four quarter notes.

6. Draw four half notes.

7. Draw four dotted half notes.

8. Draw four whole notes.

9. Draw a ♡ for every beat in the rhythm below.

10. Draw a bar line after each four beats. Draw a double bar at the end.

11. This sign :‖ is called a _____ sign.

   It means to _____.

22

# Introducing the White Keys

Each of the white keys has a letter name.

# A  B  C  D  E  F  G

The letters repeat over and over again on the keyboard. As you go up, the letters go forward. As you go down, the letters go backward.

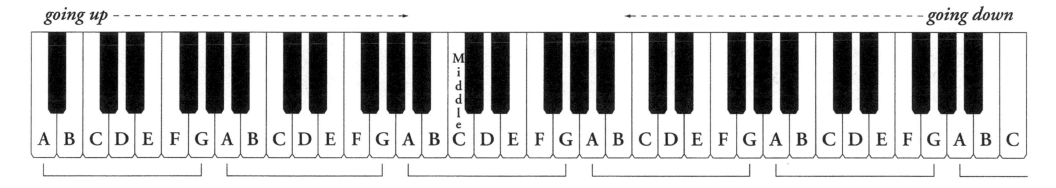

*going up* - - - - - - - - - - - - - - - - - - - - ->                    <- - - - - - - - - - - - - - - - - - - *going down*

A B C D E F G A B C D E F G A B C D E F G A B C D E F G A B C D E F G A B C

## Practice Directions

1. Using only your second or third finger, play A B C D E F G forward (going up the keyboard) and backward (going down the keyboard), saying the letters out loud as you play.  Play different groups of ABCDEFG.
2. Count the number of times you find all seven keys on your piano starting with the lowest key. How many?_____

23

The keys C D E are neighbors of the two-black-key set.

C D E

The keys F G A B are neighbors of the three-black-key set.

F G A B

## Practice Directions

1. Play each C D E on the piano. Start at the low end of the keyboard with your left hand. At the middle, change to your right hand. Say each letter as you play.
2. Play each F G A B on the piano using the same directions as above.
3. Sing the note names as you play.
4. Sing the words as you play.

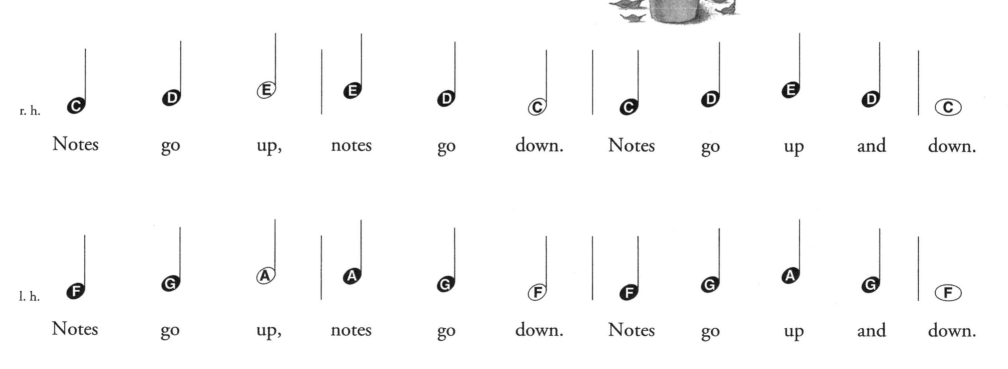

r. h.  C     D     E     E     D     C     C     D     E     D     C

Notes    go    up,    notes    go    down.    Notes    go    up    and    down.

l. h.  F     G     A     A     G     F     F     G     A     G     F

Notes    go    up,    notes    go    down.    Notes    go    up    and    down.

24

# V.I.P. Notes—G F C
## (Very Important Place Notes)

## Clef Signs

Long ago, when music was first being written down, some musicians in the Church decided to make certain notes special because they were in a very important place. One way they showed this in their music was by putting the letters on the lines of music. They called these letters clef signs.

The G clef looked like this:   As time passed, it changed to this:   and finally this: 

The F clef looked like this:   As time passed, it changed to this:   and finally this: 

There is another clef called the C clef. It is not used in piano music, but it, too, has a special place, as you will discover later.

# Very Important Place
## *The Treble Note G*

The G or treble clef shows us the location of our first V.I.P. note, G.

V.I.P. G is a "line note" because a line goes through it.

The right hand usually plays in the treble or G clef. The note just above the G is A. A is on the space above the line note G.

G or treble clef → V.I.P. G line

## Practice Directions

1. Sing "line" or "space" as you play.
2. Sing the note names as you play.
3. Count the rhythm as you play.
4. Try playing the piece with different finger groups, starting with 2, 3, or 4.

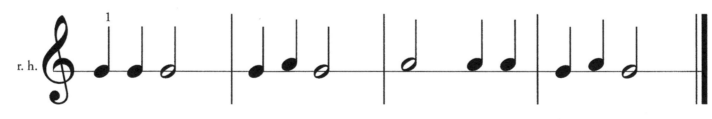

## "G" I Know

Use the practice directions above. Then, sing the words as you play.

On the tre - ble clef I go. "G" I know. "G" I know.

# Introducing Dynamics

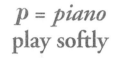 Playing music loudly or softly is called dynamics.
Signs in the music tell us how loudly or softly to play.

$\boldsymbol{f}$ = *forte*
play loudly

$\boldsymbol{p}$ = *piano*
play softly

Play the melody below using the practice directions on page 26.
Be sure to observe the $\boldsymbol{f}$ and the $\boldsymbol{p}$.

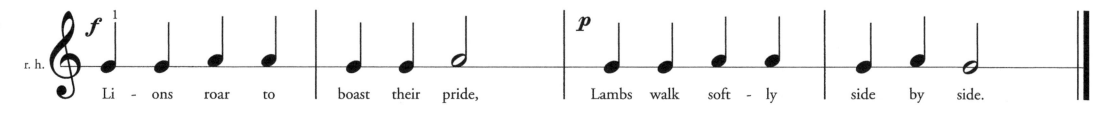

27

# Very Important Place
## *The Bass Note F*

The F or bass clef shows us the location of our next V.I.P. note, F.

V.I.P. F is also a "line note."

The left hand usually plays in the bass clef.

The note just above the F is G.

G is on the space above the "line note" F.

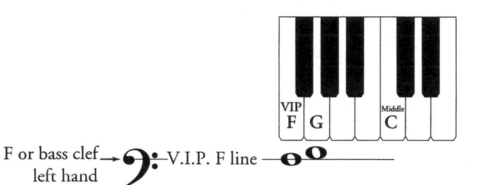

F or bass clef → left hand — V.I.P. F line

## Additional Practice Direction

Be sure to observe the $f$ and $p$.

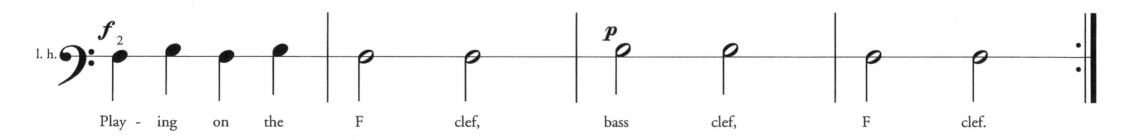

Play - ing    on    the    F    clef,    bass    clef,    F    clef.

Also practice starting with the fingers 3, 4, and 5.

# F Clef—Adding a New Line Note, A

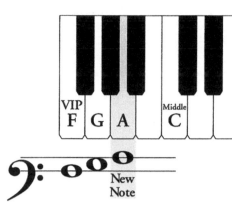

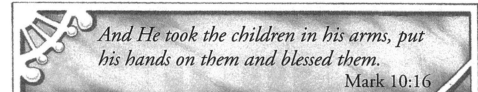

## JESUS' HANDS WERE KIND HANDS

*Words by* Margaret Cropper*

Traditional French Melody

Je - sus' hands were kind hands, do - ing good to all,
*p* Heal - ing pain and sick - ness, bless - ing chil - dren all small.

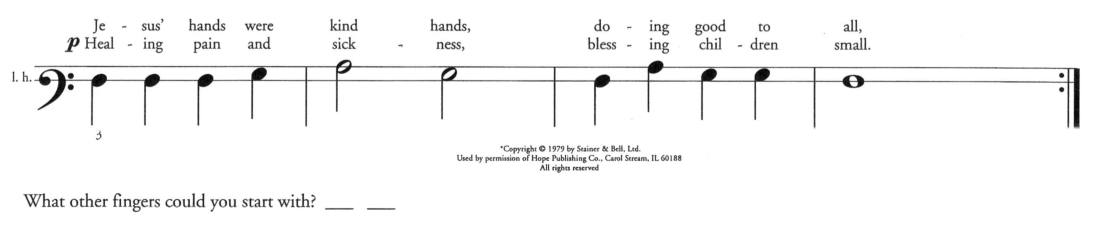

l. h.

What other fingers could you start with? ___ ___

Teacher's duet part (student part to be played as written)

29

# G Clef—Adding a New Line Note, B

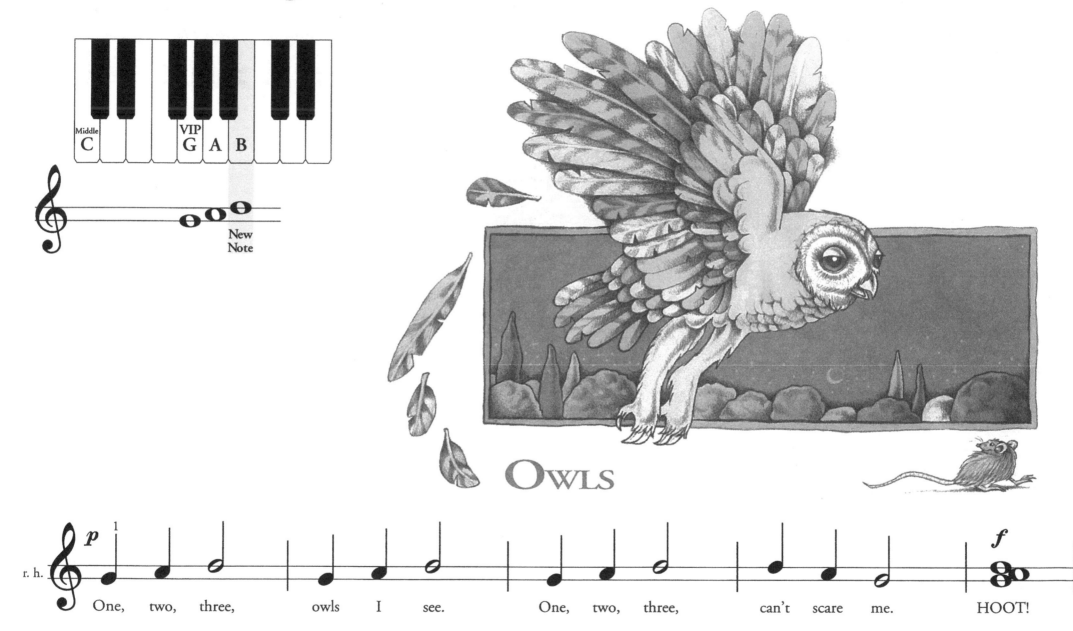

OWLS

One, two, three, owls I see. One, two, three, can't scare me. HOOT!

Also play starting with fingers 2 and 3.

# Introducing the Time Signature

The **time signature** tells how many beats are in a measure.
You can find one at the very beginning of a song.

The top **4** tells us how many beats are in each measure.
The bottom **4** tells us that a ♩ (quarter note) gets one beat.

- Find the time signature in the song *Thank You, Lord, for Music.*
- How many beats are in each measure? _____
- What kind of note gets one beat? _____

## THANK YOU, LORD, FOR MUSIC

Thank you, Lord, thank you, Lord, thank you, Lord, for mu - sic.

Thank you, Lord, thank you, Lord, thank you, Lord, for mu - sic.

Teacher's duet part (student part to be played as written)

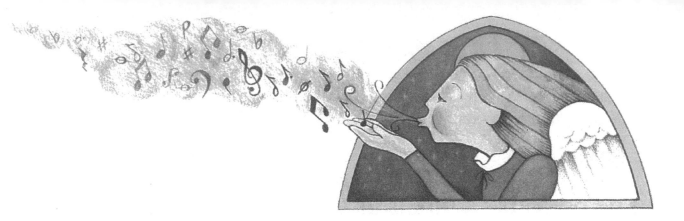

# PRAISE THE LORD WITH MUSIC

*f* Praise the Lord, *p* praise the Lord, *f* praise the Lord with mu - sic!

*f* Praise the Lord, *p* praise the Lord, *f* praise the Lord with mu - sic!

Also try starting with different fingers.
What is your favorite starting finger? ____

Teacher's duet part (student part to be played as written)

It is good to praise the Lord and make
music to your Name, O Most High.
Psalm 92:1

32

# Introducing the Five-Line Staff

A **staff** is the five lines and four spaces on which we write music.
Higher notes are on the **treble staff** and are usually played with the right hand.
We use the **G** clef on the **treble staff**.

- Find **V.I.P. G** on the treble staff below. Sing the note name as you play.

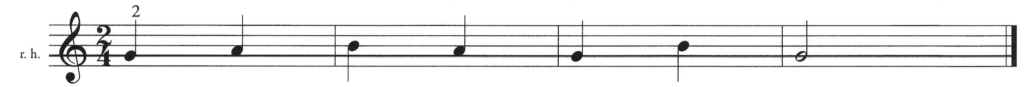

Notice the time signature. There are *two* beats in each measure. A quarter note
gets one beat.

Lower notes are on the **bass staff** and are usually played with the left hand.
We use the **F** clef on the **bass staff**.

- Find **V.I.P. F** on the bass staff below. Sing the note names as you play.

Notice the time signature. There are *three* beats in each measure.
A quarter note gets one beat. How many beats does the dotted half note get? _____

# Playing on the Five-Line Treble Staff

- Find the V.I.P. G line at the beginning of *Good News! Chariot's Coming!*
- On what note does the song begin? _____
- What other notes do you play in the song? _____
- What different finger groups could you use? _____, _____

## GOOD NEWS! CHARIOT'S COMING!

f                                        p                                        African-American Spiritual

r. h.

Good      news!      Char - iot's    com - ing!    Good      news!      Char - iot's    com - ing!

f

Good      news!      Char - iot's    com - ing!    Don't leave    me      be - hind!

Teacher's duet part (student part to be played as written)

1., 2., 3.,                    4.

f

*p* – 1st and 3rd times
*f* – 2nd and 4th times

34

# Playing on the Five-Line Bass Staff

- Find the V.I.P. F line at the beginning of *Dinosaurs.*
- On what note does the song begin?
- What other notes do you play in the song?
- What different finger groups could you use?

## DINOSAURS

Di - no - saurs, di - no - saurs, hear them rum - ble, hear them roar.

It's all right, don't be scared. They don't live here an - y - more.

Teacher's duet part (student part to be played as written)

35

# Review No. 2

1. Oops! We goofed! Can you help each letter name find the right key by drawing a line from the letter to the correct key?

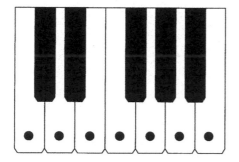

F A D G C B E

2. Fill in the missing letter names.

F ___ ___ ___          C ___ ___          ___ ___ G ___

___ B ___ ___          ___ ___ A ___          ___ ___ ___ C

___ ___ F ___ ___          D ___ ___ ___

3. Draw the correct V.I.P. note on each staff below. Name each note.

_____

_____

4. ___ is a _____ clef. It is on the _____ staff.

   The _____ hand usually plays music written on this staff.

5. ___ is a _____ clef. It is on the _____ staff.

   The _____ hand usually plays music written on this staff.

6. Playing loud or soft sounds in music is called _____.

7. 𝒇 is from the word_____and means to play

   _____.

8. 𝒑 is from the word_____and means to

   play_____.

9. Name the notes.

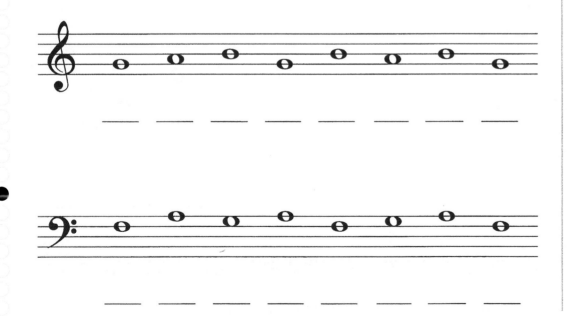

10. 𝟒/𝟒 is called a _____  _____

    The top number tells how many_____are in each

    _____.

    The bottom number tells that a quarter note gets_____beat.

11. Below the staff, write the three possible fingers you could use to

    begin this piece.

    ____

    ____

    ____

# Repeat — Step — Skip

**Repeat**

Notes that stay on the same line or space repeat.

## REPEATING

Play once with each hand. Begin on any note.

Play - ing    on    one    key,        just    one    key.

**Step**

Notes that go up or down from a line to a space or from a space to a line step.

## STEPPING

Play once with each hand. Begin on any note.

Step - ping,    step-ping up  and  step - ping,    step-ping down a - gain.

🎵 Skip

Notes that go from a line to the next line or from a space to the next space skip.

## LINE SKIPPING

Play once with each hand. Begin on any note.

r. h. 1

l. h. 5

When I skip from line to line, I don't touch an - y spac - es.

## SPACE SKIPPING

Play once with each hand. Begin on any note.

r. h. 3

l. h. 3

Notes that hide be - tween the lines, these are all called space notes.

39

# Songs with Notes that Repeat

## Woodpecker (Right Hand)

*p*
*3*

r. h. Wood - peck - er, wood - peck - er, tap - ping on a tree.

*f*

Wood - peck - er, wood - peck - er, hap - py as can be.

## Woodpecker (Left Hand)

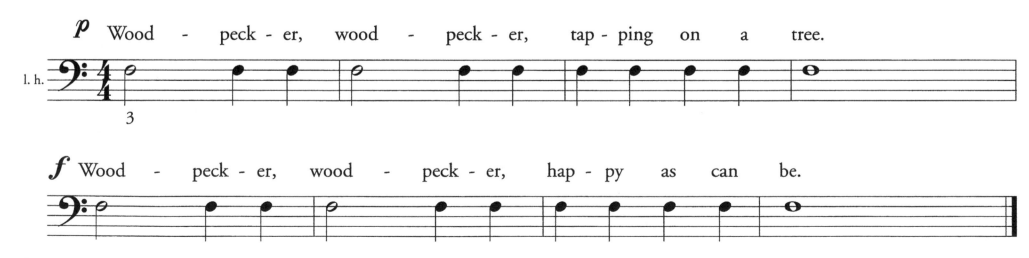

*p* Wood - peck - er, wood - peck - er, tap - ping on a tree.

l. h.

*3*

*f* Wood - peck - er, wood - peck - er, hap - py as can be.

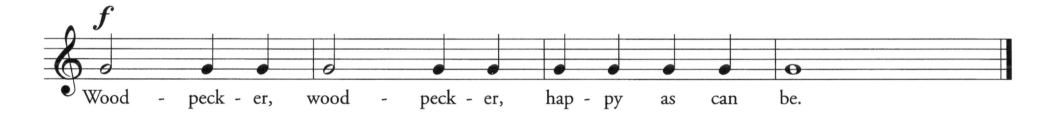

40

# Songs with Notes that Step

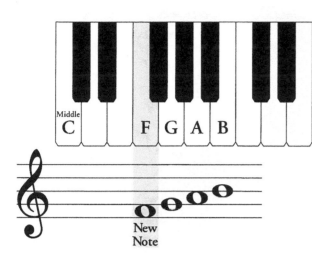

New Note

## RUSTIC DANCE

r. h.

What other finger could you use to begin? ____

Teacher's duet part (student part to be played as written)

Reminder: 𝅗𝅥. =

VIP **F G A B** Middle **C**

New Note

*Little Bird* begins one note above the V.I.P. F.
After playing *Little Bird* with the fingers given, play it again starting with the 3rd finger.

## LITTLE BIRD

Lit - tle bird in the tree, won't you sing for me?

l. h.

4

Teacher's duet part (student part to be played as written)

*play both hands 8va*

42

New Notes

*Birch Tree* begins on a neighbor note above the V.I.P. note G. It is named ____.

## BIRCH TREE

*Words by* Mark Williams

Russian Folk Melody

*f* See the love - ly birch in the mead - ow, *p* love - ly sil - ver

leaves in the mead - ow. *f* Too - ra - loo, hear the

*slowing to the end*

wind blow. *p* Too - ra - loo, hear the wind blow.

Teacher's duet part (student part to be played one octave higher)

43

# Songs with Notes that Skip

*Grandpa's House* begins on a neighbor note above V.I.P. G named_____.
Find all the skips in the piece.

## GRANDPA'S HOUSE

When you go to Grand-pa's house, you will nev - er see a mouse.

For, you see, he has a cat sleep - ing on his wel - come mat.

Teacher's duet part (student part to be played as written)

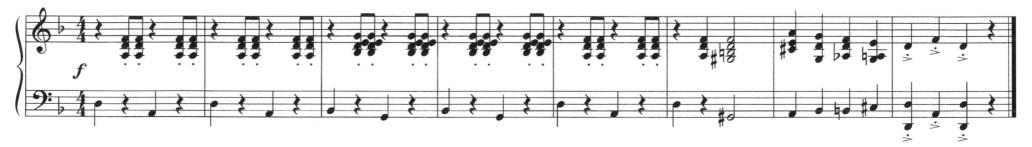

Before you play *We Three Kings,* find all the skips and steps in the song.

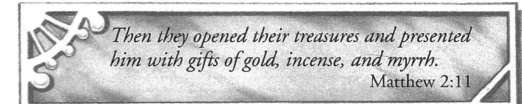

*Then they opened their treasures and presented him with gifts of gold, incense, and myrrh.*
Matthew 2:11

# WE THREE KINGS

*Words and music by*
John Henry Hopkins, Jr.
(1820–1891)

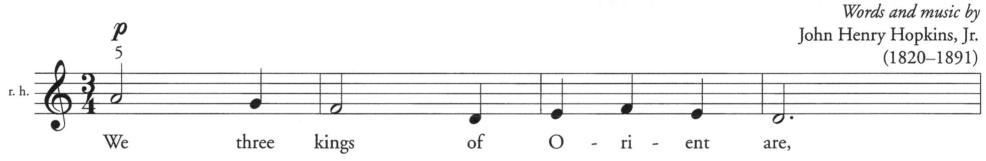

We three kings of O - ri - ent are,

bear - ing gifts we trav - el a - far.

Teacher's duet part (student part to be played one octave higher)

# Introducing Middle C
## *The New V.I.P. Note*

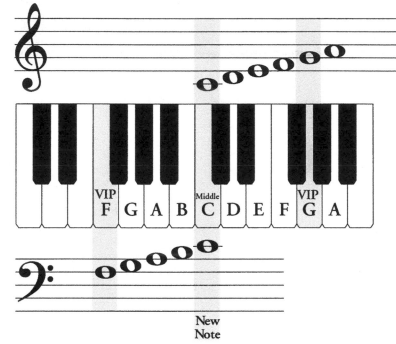

Middle C is in the middle, between the bass staff and the treble staff. To draw it, we add a small line below the treble staff, or above the bass staff. This is called a **ledger line.** On the keyboard, middle C is the same key, whether it is written below the treble staff or above the bass staff.

To find middle C on the treble staff, place your right hand 5 finger on the V.I.P. note G. Then play down the keyboard G-F-E-D-C.

To find middle C on the bass staff, place your left hand 5 finger on the V.I.P. note F. Then play up the keyboard F-G-A-B-C.

Both of your thumbs should now be on the V.I.P. middle C !

*Take My Song* uses the two V.I.P. notes, F and middle C.
1. Find and circle all the V.I.P. notes in *Take My Song.*
2. Before you play, look for all the skips and steps in the song.

# TAKE MY SONG

Lord, I ask you take my song. Help me play for you a - lone.

Lord, I put my trust in you as you lead in all I do.

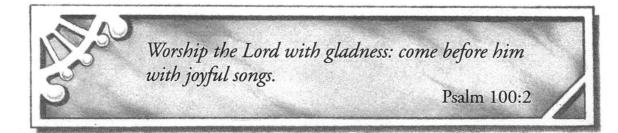

*Worship the Lord with gladness: come before him with joyful songs.*

Psalm 100:2

**Right Hand**

Middle C D E F **VIP** G

*In the Shadow of a Hill* uses two V.I.P. notes, G and middle C.

1. Find and circle all the V.I.P. notes in *In the Shadow of a Hill*.

2. Before you play the piece, find all the skips and steps in the song.

# IN THE SHADOW OF A HILL

Russian Folk Melody

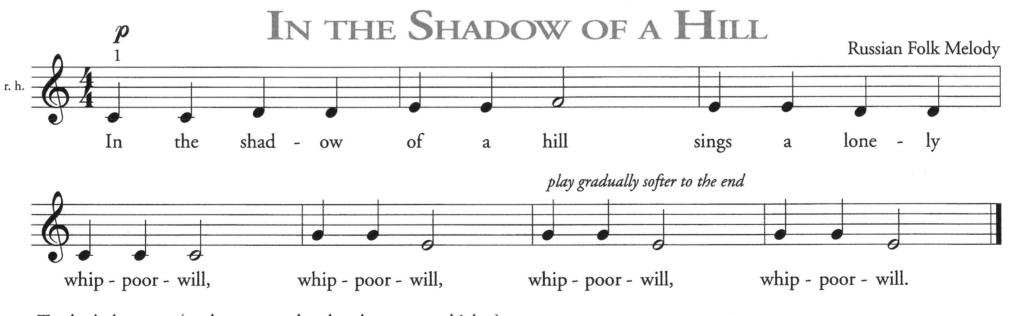

In the shad - ow of a hill sings a lone - ly

*play gradually softer to the end*

whip - poor - will, whip - poor - will, whip - poor - will, whip - poor - will.

Teacher's duet part (student part to be played one octave higher)

# TRUST IN THE LORD

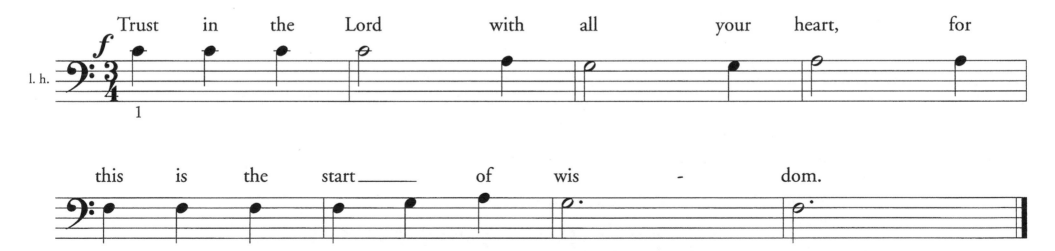

Trust in the Lord with all your heart, for this is the start of wis - dom.

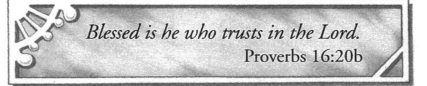

*Blessed is he who trusts in the Lord.*
Proverbs 16:20b

# OLD TEDDY BEAR

Tip - toe soft - ly up the stairs; please don't wake the Ted - dy Bear.

High - er, high - er to the sky; poor old Ted - dy starts to cry.

*slowing to the end*

Soft - ly, now, with voice so sweet sing old Ted - dy back to sleep.

Teacher's duet part (student plays as written)

*play r.h. 8va higher*

*slowing*

# LOUDLY SOUND THE TRUMPET

Loud - ly sound the trum - pet! Shake the tam - bour - ine!

Lift your voice, all re - joice! Glad ho - san - nas ring!

*Praise him with the sounding of the trumpet... praise him with the tambourine... Let everything that has breath praise the Lord.*

Psalm 150:3-6

51

# JACK AND JILL

Jack and Jill went up the hill to fetch a pail of wa - ter.

Jack fell down and broke his crown, and Jill came tum - bling af - ter.

# EVEN IN THE DARK OF NIGHT

E - ven in the dark of night, Lord, I know you see me.

l. h.

How your love is shin - ing bright. In your arms you keep me.

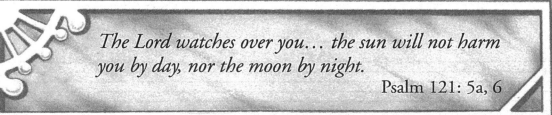

*The Lord watches over you... the sun will not harm you by day, nor the moon by night.*

Psalm 121: 5a, 6

# Introducing the Grand Staff

The treble staff and bass staff are usually connected together in piano music. This is called a grand staff. Each grand staff begins with a brace and a bar line.

## Practice Directions:

1. Look at the grand staff below. Circle the V.I.P. notes F, C, and G. (Remember: The V.I.P. note C can be written on either staff and is played by the same key on the piano.)
2. Draw a box around the notes the left hand plays. Draw another box around the notes the right hand plays.
3. Put both thumbs on middle C. Play all the notes shown on the grand staff below. starting with the F (bass) clef note F. Play middle C once with each 1 finger.

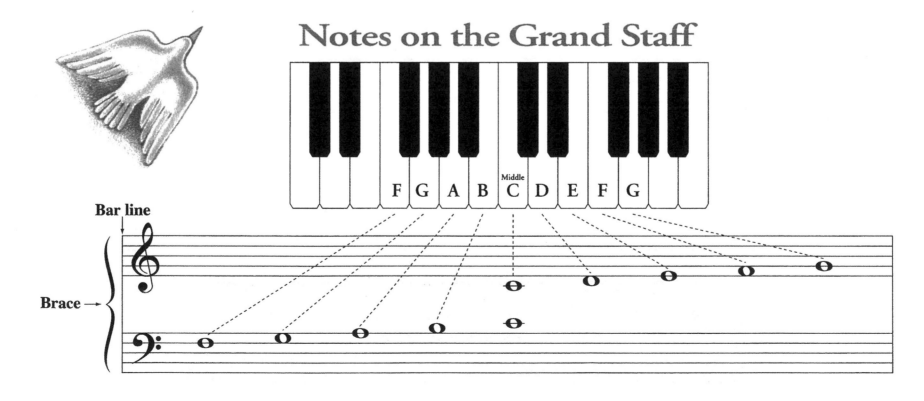

## Notes on the Grand Staff

# The Lamb and the Lion

*p* Soft - ly walks the lit - tle lamb in the mead - ow green.

*f* Loud - ly roars the might - y lion; he's the jung - le king!

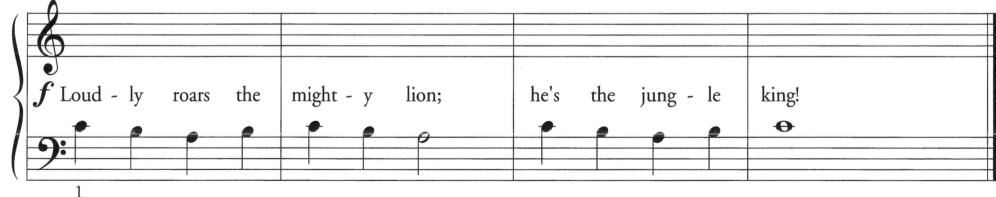

*Behold the Lamb of God, who takes away the sin of the world.* John 1:29

*...See, the lion of the tribe of Judah...* Revelation 5:5

# Bingo

Lively

American Folk Song

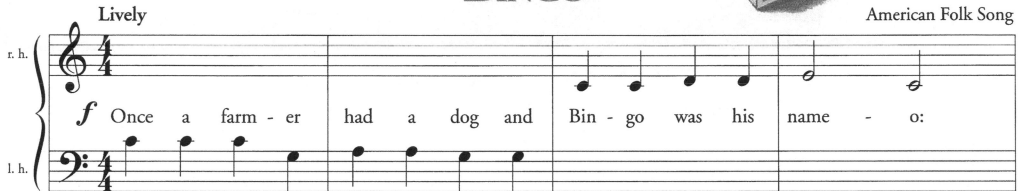

*f* Once a farm-er had a dog and Bin-go was his name - o:

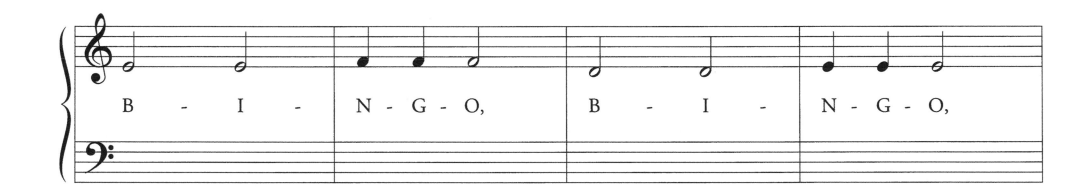

B - I - N - G - O, B - I - N - G - O,

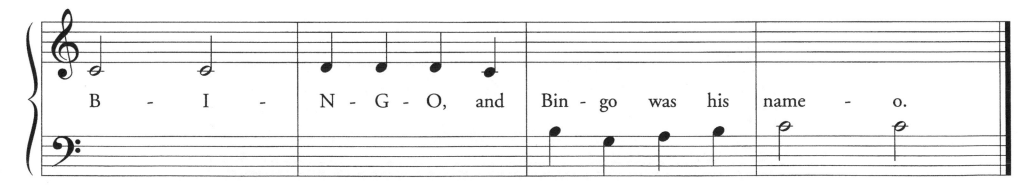

B - I - N - G - O, and Bin-go was his name - o.

# WE ARE CLIMBING JACOB'S LADDER

African-American Spiritual

# PRELUDE*

**Sadly**

*p* Long be-fore a storm be-gins, you can hear the thun-der call.

Long be-fore the win-ter wind, you can hear its song in fall.

*Optional ending*

You can hear its song in fall. *softer* Oo.

*A prelude is a piece designed to be played before another piece or event, but it often stands alone.

# COME, CHRISTIANS, JOIN TO SING

*Words by* Christian H. Bateman
(1813–1889)

Spanish Melody

# Review No. 3

1. Circle step, skip, or repeat for each measure.

step  skip  repeat    step skip repeat    step skip repeat    step skip repeat    step skip repeat    step skip repeat    step skip repeat

2. In each measure, draw two more notes that follow the
   same pattern of step, skip, or repeat.

3. Draw the notes on the staff. Use quarter notes.

G  F  A  B  E  G  D  C      F  A  B  G  C  A  F  G

4. Fill in the top number of each time signature with the number of
   beats in the measure.

5. Draw and name the V.I.P. notes F, C, and G on the grand staff.
   Use dotted half notes.

6. Circle the dynamic marking that fits best with each picture.

*piano*   *forte*        *piano*   *forte*        *piano*   *forte*        *piano*   *forte*        *piano*   *forte*

61

# Music Dictionary

| | | |
|---|---|---|
| Bar or bar line | \| | separates the notes in one measure from those in another measure |
| Brace | { | connects treble staff and bass staff together to form a Grand staff |
| Dynamics | | loud and soft playing in music |
| Double bar | ‖ | used to show the end of a song |
| F clef | 𝄢 | used to show lower notes. Also called the bass clef. |
| *Forte* | *f* | play loudly |
| G clef | 𝄞 | used to show the higher notes. Also called the treble clef |
| Grand staff | | the treble staff and bass staff connected together by a brace and a bar line |

| | | |
|---|---|---|
| Measure | | the notes and rests contained between two bars (bar lines) |
| *Piano* | *p* | play softly |
| Repeat sign | ꞉‖ | play again from the beginning |
| Rhythm | | the combination of long and short tones in music |
| Staff | | five lines and four spaces upon which music is written |
| Time signature | $\frac{3}{4}$ $\frac{2}{4}$ $\frac{4}{4}$ *etc.* | tells how many beats are in a measure and what kind of note equals one beat |
| V. I. P. notes | | Very Important Place notes |

# Certificate of Achievement

## This Certifies that

### has successfully completed

# *Keys for the Kingdom*™
*Level A*

### and is promoted to Level B

TEACHER:

DATE: